Index

Affordable, portable and beautiful. Create a beaded necklace in every color.

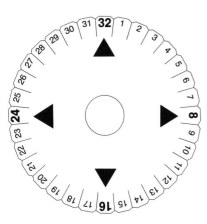

Braiding Wheel

An inexpensive foam wheel is available at most craft shops in the bead or plastic lace department. This wheel works well.

A larger and thicker foam wheel makes braiding even easier. The thicker the foam, the better it will hold the yarns and cords.

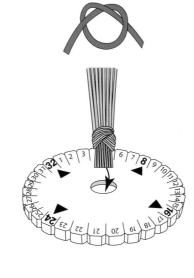

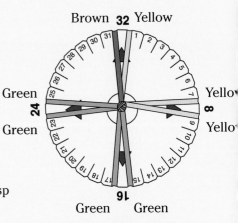

OR

Overhand Knot

Hold one end of all cords evenly. Tie an Overhand Knot.

Center Hole

Push the knot into the center hole to the back of wheel. Spread threads across the surface of the wheel and insert them into the slots.

A Word About Tension

Your finished project will look better when you maintain a steady tension on the cords as you move around the wheel.

Keep the cord laying flat across the wheel.

Keep the Overhand Knot in the center of the hole as you work.

Bobbins

Bobbins make braiding easier and help keep the threads from tangling.

Wrap cords around the bobbins, secure them with rubber bands.

Wrap a bobbin for each cord that has no beads. If the cord requires beads, string beads before wrapping the end on bobbin.

Bracelets

Next time you need a quick gift or you want to do a fun craft, try these simple friendship bracelets.

BRACELET INSTRUCTIONS:
Braiding:
Use a double strand in each bobbin.
Refer to the Set-Up diagram.
Follow the instructions for a Round Braid on page 5.
Finish:
Refer to Finishing instructions on page 6.

Three Color Bracelet

SIZE: 9"
MATERIALS:
Four 30" strands of
   Green pearl cotton
Three 30" strands of
    Yellow pearl cotton
One 30" strand of
   Brown pearl cotton
2 end cones • Toggle clasp
Two 2mm round beads
Two 6" lengths of
   20 gauge wire

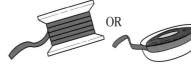

Braiding Wheel Set-Up
for Three Color Bracelet

Green & Yellow Bracelet

SIZE: 8"
MATERIALS:
Four 30" strands of
   Green pearl cotton
Four 30" strands of
    Yellow pearl cotton
2 end cones • Toggle clasp
Two 2mm round beads
Two 6" lengths of
   20 gauge wire

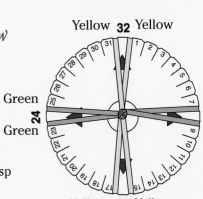

Braiding Wheel Set-Up
for Green & Yellow Bracelet

How to Get Started

Round Braid

In this style of braid, the numbers change position as the wheel rotates in a counterclockwise direction.

Begin with #32 at the Top.

1. Always start with the bottom left strand
(between 16 & 17).
Place it to the left of the top strands (between 30 & 31).

2. There are now 3 strands on top.

3. Pull out the right strand at the top
(between 1 & 32).
Insert it to the right of the bottom strands (between 14 & 15).
Turn the Wheel Counterclockwise.
Eight is now at the Top.

4. Pick up the bottom left lace
(between 24 & 25).
Place it in the slot to the left of the top lace (between 6 & 7).
Pick up the top right lace (between 8 & 9).
Place it in the slot to the right of the bottom lace (between 22 & 23).
Turn the Wheel Counterclockwise.
Sixteen is now at the top

5. Repeat until you reach the desired length.

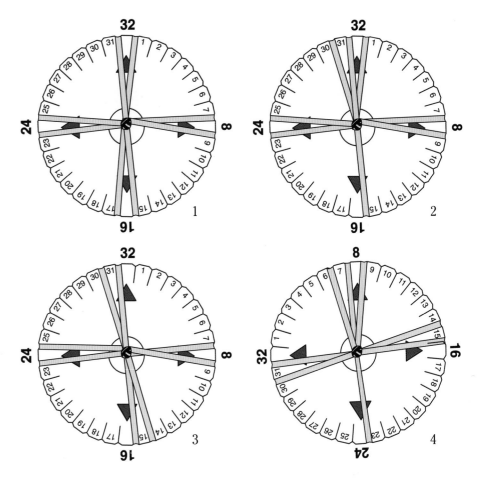

Cord Length

To determine the length of cord needed for a necklace, multiply the desired finished length by 3.

> Example: If you want a 20" necklace, each cord must be 60" long (that's 5 feet EACH).
> Note: All 8 strands need not be the same cord.
> Mix colors, textures and thicknesses as desired.
> Begin with all cords the same length.

Setting Up the Wheel

All projects begin in the same manner.

The Set Up Diagram:
The slot between #32 and #1 is the top.
Position wheel with #32 at the top.

Numbered Slots:
Slot #1 is between #32 and number #1.
Note: A slot is actually to the left of the number indicated.

Tip for Stopping

We all have interruptions - someone knocks at the door, the dog wants to go out, or it's time to do something else.

Keep track of where you stopped with this tip.

Before you set your wheel down, always stop at Step 2, with 3 strands at the top. When you pick up your braiding again, you will know exactly what part of the wheel is at the top and you will be able to resume without any trouble.

Working with Beads

Beads make any cord behave as though it is a thick cord, so the beads will show on the outside of the cord.

After setting up your wheel, add beads to some strands following the instructions for your project.

Never place a bead in the slot. When you move the string with the beads, push 1 bead into position before sliding the cord into its assigned slot.

Pendants

There are several ways to add pendants to your necklace.

The simplest is to thread the pendant onto your necklace before attaching the end cap.

An option is to sew the pendant to the cord with thread and a needle. Choose a thread color that matches the necklace, hide knots inside the braid.

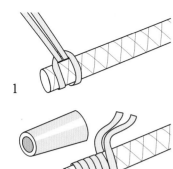

1

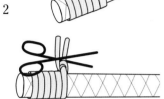

2

How to Finish

Insert the ends into an 'end cap' or 'cone' and secure with a wrapped loop for a beautiful professional look.

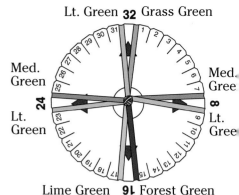

Lt. Green **32** Grass Green

Med. Green   Med. Gree

Lt. Green   **24**   **8**   Lt. Gree

Lime Green **9ㄴ** Forest Green

Braiding Wheel Set-Up
for Square Pendant

Check the length of your necklace.

If the necklace is too long,
cut off some braid length.
If the necklace is too short,
continue braiding.

3

4

1. **Fold 24" of thread** in half to form a loop.

Pass the tails through the loop and pull the thread tight. Wrap the thread several times close to the cinch point binding the threads tightly so they fit easily into the end cone.

2. **Wrap a length** slightly less than the length end conebead cap so the wrapping does not show.

3. **Tie several knots** at the end and trim the loose tails close to the binding.

4. **Repeat for the other end**, binding right above the Overhand Knot. Cut off the Overhand Knot.

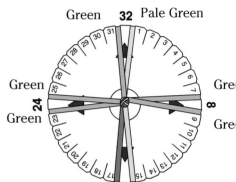

Green **32** Pale Green

Green   Gre

Green   **24**   **8**   Gre

Med. Green **9ㄴ** Pale Green
- Add beads

Braiding Wheel Set-Up
for Swirling Glass Pendant

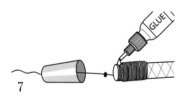

5

5. **Add a pendant** to the necklace now, if desired.

6. **Wrap a 6" piece of wire** securely around the end of each binding.

7. **Spread glue** on a wrapped end, covering the end thoroughly, and insert the end into an end cone.

Purple **32** Purple

Green   Purp

Green   **24**   **8**   Purp

Green **9ㄴ** Green

Braiding Wheel Set-Up
for Abalone Shell Pendant

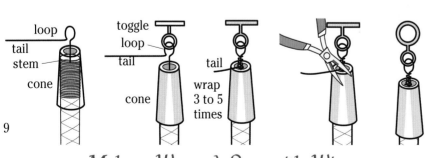

6

7

8. **Push end** cone onto the cord securely.
Repeat for the other end.
Let glue dry for 24 hours.

9. **Secure the end** by adding a toggle clasp and making a wrapped loop with wire.

8

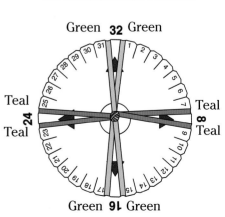

loop
tail
stem
cone

toggle
loop
tail
cone

tail
wrap
3 to 5
times

Green **32** Green

Teal   Teal

Teal   **24**   **8**   Teal

Green **9ㄴ** Green

Braiding Wheel Set-Up
for Round Glass Pendant

9

Make a Wrapped Loop with Wire

1. Shape a loop and form tail into a 90° angle. • 2. Slip a toggle clasp onto the loop. • 3. Tightly wrap the tail around the wire stem 3 to 5 times until it is snug. Cut off the tail with wire cutters. • 4. Repeat on the other end of the cord with the other half of the toggle clasp.

Enjoy your necklace!

'It's Hip to Be Square' Pendant Necklace

SIZE: 22"

MATERIALS:

Pearl cotton - Three 70" strands of Light Green • One 70" strand of Grass Green
• One 70" strand of Forest Green • Two 70" strands of Medium Green
One 70" strand of Lime Green chenille yarn • Glass pendant
2 end cones • Toggle clasp • 3" head pin • Two 6" lengths of 20 gauge wire
Green beads - One 13mm faceted, one 6mm faceted • One 4mm round bead

INSTRUCTIONS - see basic instructions on pages 4 - 6.

Pendant: Place beads on a head pin: 6mm - glass - 13mm - 4mm.
Attach to cord with a wrapped loop of wire.

'Swirling Glass' Pendant Necklace

SIZE: 26½"

MATERIALS:

Pearl cotton - Fifteen 85" strands of Green • Six 85" strands of Pale Green • Three
85" strands of Medium Green • Glass Swirl pendant
200 iridescent Blue/Purple size 8 "E" beads • 6" of 19-strand beading wire
2 end cones • Toggle clasp • Two 6" lengths of 20 gauge wire

INSTRUCTIONS - see basic instructions on pages 4 - 6.

Braiding: Use 3 strands on each bobbin.
Thread beads onto 1 strand of Med. Green.

Pendant: String 17 beads and a crimp bead onto 6" of 19-strand beading
wire. Pass through the hole in pendant. Wrap around braided cord,
passing ends through the crimp bead. Pull taut, crimp, trim excess wire.

'Abalone Shell' Pendant Necklace

SIZE: 25"

MATERIALS:

Pearl cotton - Four 80" strands of Green • Three 80" strands of Purple
One 80" strand of metallic Purple rat tail cord • Abalone shell pendant
2 end cones • Toggle clasp • Two 6" lengths of 24 gauge wire

INSTRUCTIONS - see basic instructions on pages 4 - 6.

Pendant: String pendant onto the center of the cord.

'Round Glass' Pendant Necklace

SIZE: 19"

MATERIALS:

Pearl cotton - Eight 70" strands of Green • Eight 70" strands of Teal
Glass pendant • 7-strand beading wire • Two 5mm round beads
• 3 potato pearls • *Swarovski* Turquoise bicones (6mm, 4mm)
Swarovski Indicolite bicones (4mm) - 2 of each • Crimp bead
2 end cones • Toggle clasp • Two 6" lengths of 20 gauge wire

INSTRUCTIONS - see basic instructions on pages 4 - 6.

Braiding: Use 2 strands of pearl cotton on each bobbin.

Pendant: String the following on beading wire: Pearl - 4mm Turquoise
- 2 Silver balls - 4mm Turquoise - Pearl - 6mm Turquoise - 4mm Indicolite -
Pearl - 4mm Indicolite - 6mm Turquoise - crimp bead.
Pass the bail through the hole in the glass pendant. Feed ends of the wire
back through 4 beads each. Clamp the crimp bead to secure. String the
necklace through the bail.

BASIC INSTRUCTIONS:

Braiding: Refer to the Set-Up diagram.
Follow the instructions for a Round Braid on page 5.

Finish: Refer to Finishing instructions on page 6.

Pendant Necklaces

*Gorgeous pendants deserve to be
seen. Show off your collection with braided
cords that complement the sparkling colors
unique to each pendant.*

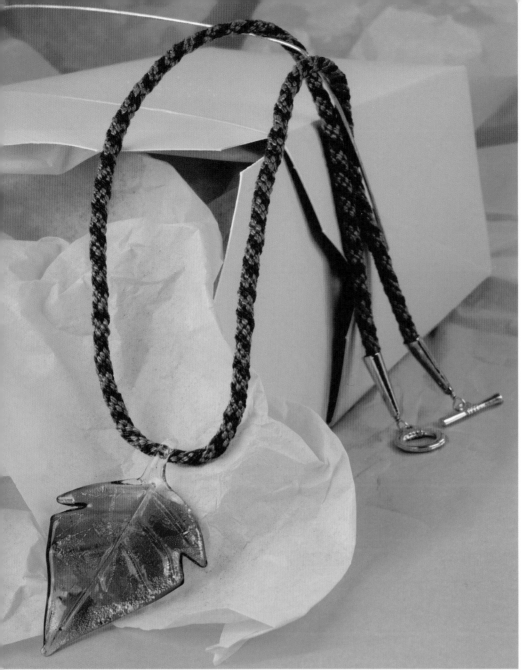

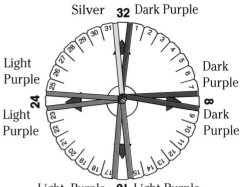

Silver **32** Dark Purple

Light Purple

Light Purple **24**

Dark Purple

Dark Purple **8**

Light. Purple **91** Light Purple

Braiding Wheel Set-Up
for Butterfly Necklace

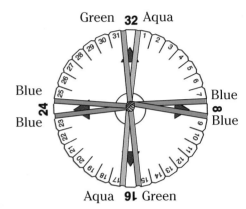

Green **32** Aqua

Blue

Blue **24**

Blue

Blue **8**

Aqua **91** Green

Braiding Wheel Set-Up
for Aqua Dreams

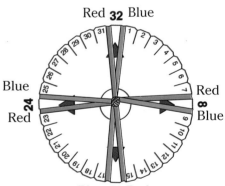

Red **32** Blue

Blue

Red **24**

Red

Blue **8**

Blue **91** Red

Braiding Wheel Set-Up
for Touch of India

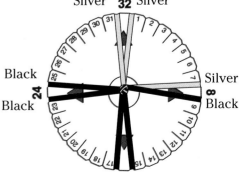

Silver **32** Silver

Black

Black **24**

Silver

Black **8**

Black **91** Black

Braiding Wheel Set-Up
for Silver Starfish

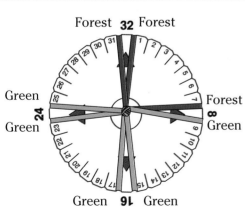

Forest **32** Forest

Green

Green **24**

Forest **8**

Green

Green **91** Green

Braiding Wheel Set-Up

Verdant Pleasures

There is nothing like a walk in the woods to refresh your soul. Capture the spirit of a leafy forest with this piece.

SIZE: 22" necklace

MATERIALS:
Six 80" strands of Forest Green pearl cotton
Ten 80" strands of Grass Green pearl cotton
Glass leaf pendant
2 end cones • Toggle clasp
Two 6" lengths of 20 gauge wire

INSTRUCTIONS:
Braiding:
Place 2 strands in each slot.
Refer to Set-Up diagram.
Follow instructions for a Round Braid on page 5.
Pendant: Thread pendant onto the cord.
Finish:
Refer to Finishing instructions on page 6.

Butterfly in Flight

Let your creativity take flight! Bright and beautiful, your spirit will soar with this sparkling pendant.

SIZE: 21" necklace

MATERIALS:
One 70" strand of Silver rat tail cord • Pearl cotton - Eight 70" strands of Lt.Purple - Six 70" strands of Dk.Purple • Crystal butterfly pendant • 2 end cones • Toggle clasp
20 gauge wire - Two 6" lengths for clasp - Two 8" lengths for pendant

INSTRUCTIONS - see basic instructions on pages 4 - 6.
Braiding: Use double strands of pearl cotton in each slot.
Pendant: Wrap the hooks on the back of the pendant with 8" wire. Pass the wire through the braid and back into the hook. Wrap securely. Trim wire tails.

Aqua Dreams

Soft sky blue and gentle green give this necklace a soothing, serene attitude.

SIZE: 26" necklace

MATERIALS:
Pearl cotton - Two 80" strands of Green - Eight 80" strands of Blue
Two 80" strands of Aqua fuzzy yarn • Glass pendant
2 end cones • Toggle clasp • Three 6" of 20 gauge wire

INSTRUCTIONS - see basic instructions on pages 4 - 6.
Braiding: Use double strands of Blue pearl cotton.
Pendant: Thread pendant onto 6" wire. Form a wrapped loop and attach to the center of the necklace cord with another wrapped loop. Wrap extra yarn around the wire, completely hiding it. Tie off yarn on the back side.

Touch of India

Bring a bit of the mystery into your accessory wardrobe. Tiny bells dangle freely.

SIZE: 18" necklace

MATERIALS:
Four 60" strands of Red craft yarn • Four 60" strands of Blue pearl cotton
2 end cones • Toggle clasp
Silver pendant • 16 Coral size 8 beads • 6 Coral 2mm rondelles
2 Coral/Blue 2mm drop bead • Three 14mm disks
20 gauge wire - Two 6" lengths for clasp - 10" for bail

INSTRUCTIONS - see basic instructions on pages 4 - 6.
Pendant: Loop the 10" wire through the pendant. Thread both ends of the wire through a Silver disk. Spread the wires apart. On each wire, string 9 assorted beads. Twist the wires together at the top and wrap around the necklace cord. Trim excess wire. Cover the wire with Blue pearl cotton.

'Silver Starfish'

Nothing is more wearable than the combination of black and silver to dress up your day.

SIZE: 17½" necklace

MATERIALS:
Three 60" strands of Silver/Black rat tail cord • Five 60" strands of Black pearl cotton • Silver Starfish pendant
2 end cones • Toggle clasp • Two 6" lengths of 20 gauge wire

INSTRUCTIONS - see basic instructions on pages 4 - 6.
Pendant: Thread pendant onto the necklace cord.

Pendants

A beautiful pendant makes a necklace special. Choose colors of cord to match the focal piece.

BASIC INSTRUCTIONS:
Braiding: Refer to Set-Up diagram.
Follow the instructions for a Round Braid on page 5.
Finish: Refer to Finishing instructions on page 6.

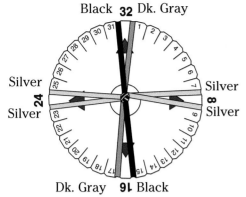

Black **32** Dk. Gray

Silver **24**

Silver

Silver **8** Silver

Dk. Gray **16** Black

Braiding Wheel Set-Up

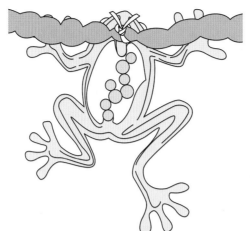

Hoppy Days

Some jewelry pieces are 'just for fun'. This character pendant leaps with twinkling whimsy guaranteed to brighten your day.

SIZE: 22"

MATERIALS:
Four 80" strands of Silver rat tail cord
Two 80" strands of Black rat tail cord
Two 80" strands of Dark Gray chenille yarn
Silver frog pendant, 45mm x 60mm
2 end cones • Toggle clasp
Two 6" lengths of 20 gauge wire

INSTRUCTIONS:
Braiding:
Refer to Set-Up diagram.
Follow the instructions for a Round Braid on page 5.
Pendant:
Tie the frog to the cord with yarn.
Tie a tight knot behind the frog.
Finish:
Refer to the Finishing instructions on page 6.

A Touch of Jazz

Jazz up your jeans with unique jewelry. Boldly colored glass pendants give this eye-catching necklace sassy appeal while the necklace is perfect for a casual day or evening.

SIZE: 20"

MATERIALS:
Two 80" strands
   of Red chenille cord
Two 80" strands
   of Turquoise eyelash yarn
Two 80" strands
   of Gold rat tail cord
Two 80" strands
   of Black rat tail cord
Red glass pendant
Black glass pendant
2 end cones • Toggle clasp
Three 8" lengths
   of 20 gauge wire

INSTRUCTIONS:
Braiding:
Refer to Set-Up diagram.
Follow the instructions for a
Round Braid on page 5.
Pendant:
Fold one 8" wire in half,
forming a loop to wrap
around necklace cord.
Attach the pendants.
Cover the wire with yarn.
Finish:
Refer to the Finish
instructions on page 6.

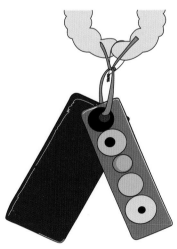

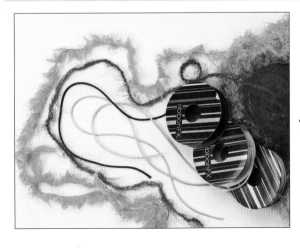

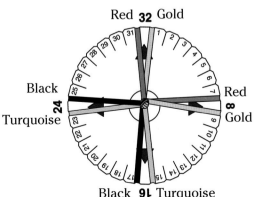

Braiding Wheel Set-Up

Ice Queen

*Twinkling beads and textures
make this necklace a real beauty.
The soft colors will brighten any day.*

SIZE: 24"

MATERIALS:
Eight 80" strands of White pearl cotton
Eight 80" strands of beading thread
36" string of Crystal bead chips
Crystal/Pink glass pendant
2 end cones • Toggle clasp
20 gauge wire - Four 12" lengths for bail & clasp
Round pencil or dowel rod

INSTRUCTIONS:

Braiding:
Refer to Set-Up diagram.

Bead Pillars:
The holes in the beads are too small to use
pearl cotton. Use strong beading thread and a
needle to string the beads. Pair each 80" bead-
ed string with an 80" strand of pearl cotton.
String 30 beads per strand.
Braid this necklace in sections.
Follow instructions for a Round Braid on page 5.
Begin by braiding 7" of cord.
Then braid a section in which you drop a bead
on every string using 15 beads per string
(half of the beads). This section will be
about 2" long.
Braid 3$\frac{1}{2}$" - 4" without beads for the pendant.
Braid another beaded section using the
remaining beads (about 2" long).
End by braiding another 7" of cord.

Finish:
Refer to Finishing instructions on page 6.

Pendant Bail:
Thread the pendant onto a wire loop.
Beginning at the center, twist the 12" wire
together, leaving 1$\frac{1}{2}$" untwisted on each end
to form a loop for the pendant to hang.
Attach wire to the necklace by wrapping
each end around the cord.
Curl the wire tails with Round pliers for an
attractive end that will not snag clothing.

White **32** White

White

24 White

White

White **8** White

White **16** White

Braiding Wheel Set-Up

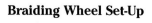

Bead Selection

Choosing your beads is as much fun as choosing your fibers. Knowing what to look for in a bead will make it easier for you to braid and give a fabulous result.

Beads that are too large stick out and distort the braid. Beads that are too small tend to disappear in the fibers. Size 6 and 8 seed beads, and "E" beads look good and create a braid that fits easily through the center hole in the wheel, even if you have a bead on each bobbin. Choose a brand with large, uniform holes.

If you prefer beads with smaller holes, such as pearls, string them on thread and pair the thread with your necklace fiber, loading the fiber and thread in the same slot.

Beads can be strung on any number of bobbins. Using 1 beaded bobbin creates space between the beads.

Look of a bead crochet rope - Set up 8 beaded bobbins and drop a bead into position with every move of the cord.

Purple Heartstrings

Purple is a regal color. Add the sparkle of silver and you have a necklace fit for a princess.

SIZE: 18"

MATERIALS:
Two 65" strands of Purple iridescent rat tail cord
Two 65" strands of Silver iridescent rat tail cord
One 65" strand of Magenta yarn
One 65" strand of Medium Purple yarn
Two 65" strands of Dark Purple yarn
Two 2mm round beads
2 end cones • Toggle clasp
Two 4" lengths of 24 gauge wire

INSTRUCTIONS:
Braiding:
Refer to Set-Up diagram.
Follow instructions for a Round Braid on page 5.

Pendant: Thread pendant onto the necklace.

Finish:
Refer to the Finishing instructions on page 6.

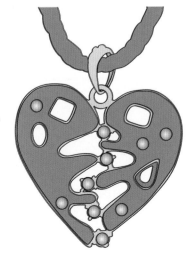

Braiding Wheel Set-Up

Rose Blush

Are you looking for something light and airy yet stylish?

Rose Blush brushes white textures with the slightest tinge of pink for a combination that is as appealing as an English tea rose.

SIZE: 22"

MATERIALS:
Four 80" strands of White chenille yarn
Two 80" strands of Pink eyelash yarn
Two 80" strands of Silver cord
30 White 4mm beads
14 White 6mm beads
3 White 18mm disks
2 end cones • Toggle clasp
Two 6" lengths of 20 gauge wire
Beading wire • 2 Crimp beads

INSTRUCTIONS:

Braiding:
Refer to Set-Up diagram.
Follow instructions for a Round Braid on page 5.

Dangles:
Feed the beading wire through the necklace cord 9½" from one end. Crimp the end to secure.

Thread the following:
  Side dangles:
    4mm - 6mm - two 4mm - 6mm - 4mm - Disk - 4mm - 6mm - two 4mm - 6mm - 4mm.
    Feed the wire in and out of the cord.
  Center dangle:
    4mm - 6mm - two 4mm - 6mm - three 4mm - 6mm - 4mm - Disk - 4mm - 6mm - three 4mm - 6mm - two 4mm - 6mm - 4mm.
    Feed wire back in and out of cord.
    Repeat a side dangle.
Feed the beading wire through the necklace cord. Crimp the end to secure.

Finish:
Refer to the Finishing instructions on page 6.

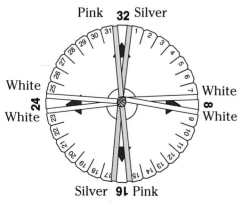

Pink **32** Silver

White **24**
White

White **8**
White

Silver **16** Pink

Braiding Wheel Set-Up

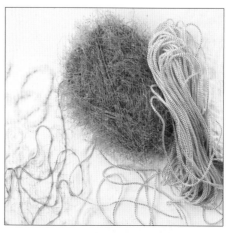

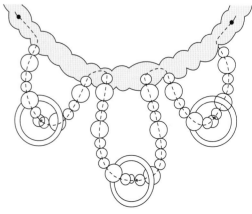

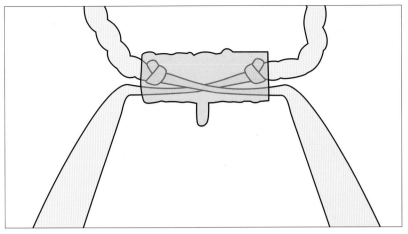

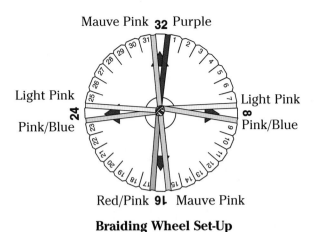

Mauve Pink **32** Purple

Light Pink
24
Pink/Blue

Light Pink
8
Pink/Blue

Red/Pink **91** Mauve Pink

Braiding Wheel Set-Up

Hot Pink and Fancy Free

Escape the need for a clasp with a whimsical, carefree lariat style necklace. This spirited piece features a slide pendant and frisky tassels that broadcast an energetic joy and ready-for-anything spunky attitude.

SIZE: Necklace: 34", Fringe: 6"

MATERIALS:
One 120" strand of Purple satin rat tail cord
Two 120" strands of Mauve Pink pearl cotton
Two 120" strands of Light Pink pearl cotton
Two 120" strands of Pink/Blue eyelash yarn
One 120" strand of Red-Pink satin ribbon
36mm slide pendant

INSTRUCTIONS:
Braiding:
Refer to Set-Up diagram. Leave a $6\frac{1}{2}$" tail.
Follow instructions for a Round Braid on page 5.
Finish:
Braid until each end has $6\frac{1}{2}$" of tail remaining.
Tie a secure knot at the end of each braid.
Thread the tails through the slide pendant from different directions.
Pull tails until the knots are hidden in pendant.

Rhapsody

It's easy to weave beads onto a braid! The effect is fabulous and no two necklaces will ever be alike.

SIZE: 22"
MATERIALS:
Four 80" strands
    of Gold 6-ply metallic floss
Two 80" strands
    of Royal Blue rat tail cord
Pearl cotton -
    Two 80" strands of Black
    Two 80" strands of Sky Blue
Glass pendant • Gold beading wire
Assortment of beads
2 end cones • Toggle clasp
Two 6" lengths and one 15" length
    of 24 gauge wire

INSTRUCTIONS:
Braiding:
Use 2 strands in each Gold slot.
Refer to Set-Up diagram.
Follow the instructions for a
Round Braid on page 5.
Woven Beads:
Connect one end of the 15" wire
through the braid and twist to
secure. Feed beads on wire and
shape as you go. Feed the wire
through the braid to create loops
or dangles.
Pendant:
Thread the pendant onto the cen-
ter of the wire.
Feed more beads on wire end as
you go. Twist wire end around
braid when you are finished.
Trim excess wire.
Finish:
Refer to the Finishing instructions
on page 6.

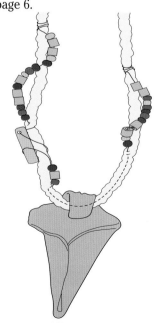

Braiding Wheel Set-Up

Royal Blue **32** Royal Blue

Gold **24**
Black

Gold **8**
Black

Sky Blue **16** Sky Blue

Braiding Wheel Set-Up

Enduring Love

Cast your love in stone with a heart pendant made of precious turquoise.

Copper eyelash fibers complement and enhance the natural lines in the stone while providing a necklace that is soft as silk - so comfortable to wear.

SIZE: 22"

MATERIALS:
Four 80" strands of Brown eyelash yarn
Eight 80" strands of Mint Green pearl cotton
Turquoise 50mm heart pendant
2 end cones • Toggle clasp
Two 6" lengths of 24 gauge wire

INSTRUCTIONS:

Braiding:
Use 2 strands pearl cotton in each Green bobbin.
Refer to Set-Up diagram.
Follow instructions for a Round Braid on page 5.

Pendant:
Thread the pendant onto the center of the cord.

Finish:
Refer to the Finishing instructions on page 6.

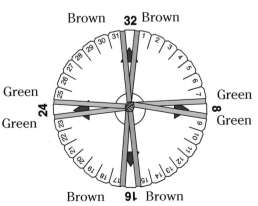

Braiding Wheel Set-Up

Braiding with Beads

The preparation for braiding with beads follows the same steps as braiding without beads.

Cut your cords in the same manner, tie an Overhand knot, and feed the tails into their assigned slots as always. The difference occurs when preparing the bobbins.

Wrap all bobbins that do not require beads first. This gets the tails out of the way and makes it easier to thread the beads.

You can only pass 1 strand through the hole of a bead. If the bead holes are large enough to accommodate your cord, string about 100 beads and wind the remaining tail onto a bobbin.

Do not be concerned about having enough beads. If you need more, simply unwind the bobbin, add more beads and rewind the bobbin.

If the holes in your beads are too small to accommodate the cord, thread them onto a matching color of silk thread. Place the thread and the cord on the bobbin together. The thread will disappear into the braid and the beads will show up beautifully.

Never place a bead in the slot. When it is time to move the beaded cord, lift the cord from its original slot, slide the bead into the center, and place the cord in its new slot. The bead will be held in place by the next cord, so continue braiding as usual.

You can braid with a bead on any number of bobbins. The procedure is always the same.

Mediterranean Waves

Beads rise and fall in gentle waves, encircling your neck in the soothing colors of sea and sky. The swirl pendant adds a refreshing promise of the seashore.

SIZE: 20½"
MATERIALS:
Eight 80" strands of Blue pearl cotton
Glass Swirl pendant
4 tubes of Blue size 6 "E" beads
Two 6" lengths of 20 gauge wire
2 end cones • Toggle clasp

INSTRUCTIONS:
Braiding:
Thread beads onto strands of all bobbins.
Refer to the Set-Up diagram.
Follow the instructions for a Round Braid on page 5.
Pendant:
Cut 2 pearl cotton threads 5" long. Pass both threads through the hole in pendant and around the necklace. Thread beads to cover the pearl cotton.
Tie a secure knot. Place a drop of bead glue on the knot and hide the knot inside a bead. Let dry.
Finish:
Do not wrap the beads. Wrap enough thread tail to fit your end cone.
Refer to the Finishing instructions on page 6.

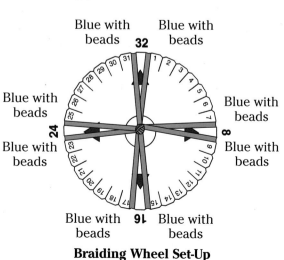

Blue with beads **32** Blue with beads
Blue with beads **24** Blue with beads **8** Blue with beads
Blue with beads Blue with beads
Blue with beads **16** Blue with beads

Braiding Wheel Set-Up